It's fun to draw Monsters, Ghosts, and Ghouls

It's fun to draw

Monsters, Ghosts, and Ghouls

Mark Bergin

Sky Pony Press
New York

Mark Bergin was born in Hastings, England. He has illustrated an award-winning series and written over twenty books. He has done many book designs, layouts, and storyboards in many styles including cartoon for numerous books, posters, and advertisements. He lives in Bexhill-on-sea with his wife and three children.

HOW TO USE THIS BOOK:
Start by following the numbered splats on the left-hand page. These steps will ask you to add some lines to your drawing. The new lines are always drawn in red so you can see how the drawing builds from step to step. Read the "You can do it!" splats to learn about drawing and coloring techniques you can use.

Sky Pony Press books may be purchased in bulk at special discounts for sales promotion, corporate gifts, fund-raising, or educational purposes. Special editions can also be created to specifications. For details, contactÂthe Special Sales Department, Sky Pony Press, 307 West 36th Street, 11th Floor, New York, NY 10018 or info@skyhorsepublishing.com.

Sky Pony® is a registered trademark of Skyhorse Publishing, Inc.®, a Delaware corporation.

Visit our website at www.skyponypress.com.

10 9 8 7 6 5 4 3 2 1

This product conforms to CPSIA 2008

Library of Congress Cataloging-in-Publication Data is available on file

Cover design by Daniel Brount
Cover illustration by Mark Bergin
ISBN: 978-1-5107-4363-2
Printed in China

Contents

Contents

It's fun to draw Monsters, Ghosts, and Ghouls

Klawz

1 Start with the head shape. Add a mouth and teeth.

2 Draw in two eyes on each side of the head, and add hair.

Splat-a-fact
Monsters have very sharp teeth and claws.

you can do it!
Use crayons to create texture and paint over with watercolor paint. Use a felt-tip marker for the lines.

3 Draw a triangle for the body, and add an oval shape. Draw in the legs.

8

4 Draw in four more legs with feet and claws.

9

Fangor

1 Start by cutting the body shape out of orange cardstock. Glue down.

2 Cut out the head and the teeth, and glue down. Draw in the eye and mouth.

MAKE SURE YOU GET AN ADULT TO HELP YOU WHEN USING SCISSORS!

you can do it!
Cut out the shapes from colored paper. Glue these onto a sheet of blue paper. Use felt-tip markers for the lines.

Splat-a-fact
This monster is very good at juggling.

3 Cut out shapes for the horns and feet, and glue down.

4 Cut out the arms and spots for the body. Glue down.

10

Fuzzbit

1 Start with this jagged shape for the head. Add one large eye.

2 Draw in the mouth, then add a jagged line for the body.

Splat-a-fact
Monsters are as strong as nine men.

You can do it!
Use a felt-tip marker for the lines. Add color with a variety of colored pencils.

3 Draw in two large feet with claws.

4 Add the arms and hands.

12

spindle

1 Start with a circle and add a mouth.

2 Draw in four eyeballs on stalks.

3 Draw in the nostrils and teeth, and add a dot to each eyeball.

you can do it!
Use a blue felt-tip marker for the lines and color in with different colored felt-tip markers.

Splat-a-fact
Some monsters are very funny and like to tell jokes.

4 Add the arms.

5 Draw in three legs.

Grunty

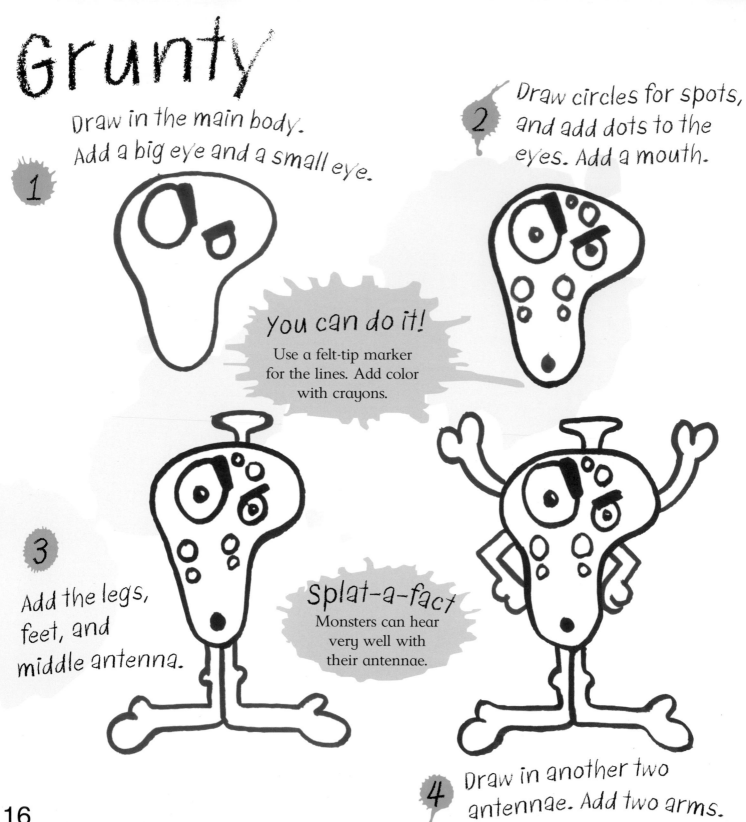

1 Draw in the main body. Add a big eye and a small eye.

2 Draw circles for spots, and add dots to the eyes. Add a mouth.

you can do it!
Use a felt-tip marker for the lines. Add color with crayons.

3 Add the legs, feet, and middle antenna.

Splat-a-fact
Monsters can hear very well with their antennae.

4 Draw in another two antennae. Add two arms.

16

17

Rangledorf

1 Draw in the spiky body.

2 Add the eyes, mouth, and teeth.

you can do it!
Use a felt-tip marker for the lines. For extra effect, paint in ink washes, adding a touch of colored ink to areas that are still wet.

splat-a-fact
Some monsters make loud, scary, roaring sounds.

3 Draw four legs.

4 Add the horns, two arms, and claws.

19

Oculus

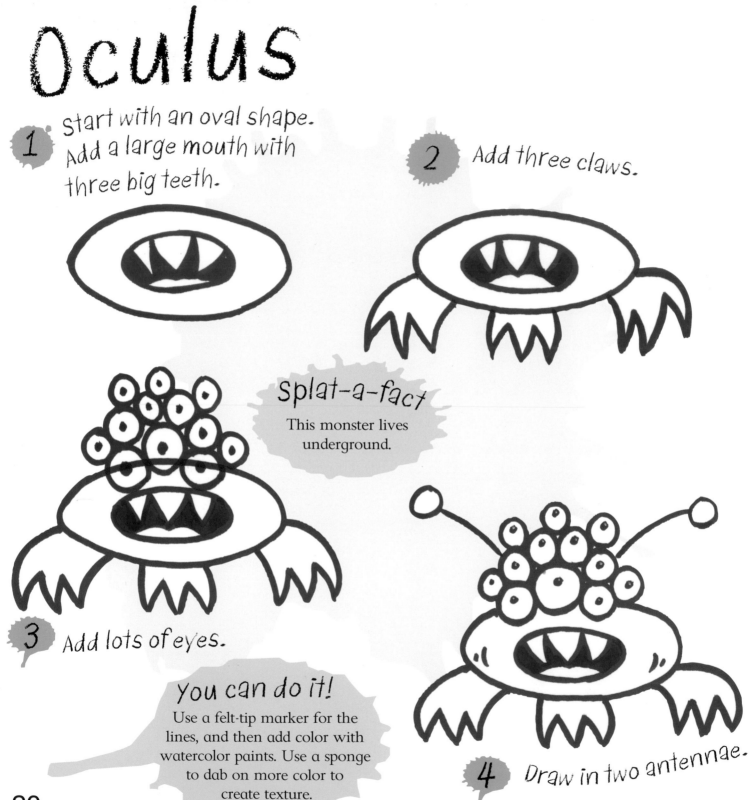

1 Start with an oval shape. Add a large mouth with three big teeth.

2 Add three claws.

3 Add lots of eyes.

splat-a-fact
This monster lives underground.

you can do it!
Use a felt-tip marker for the lines, and then add color with watercolor paints. Use a sponge to dab on more color to create texture.

4 Draw in two antennae.

20

Blarp

1 Start by drawing this shape. Add a mouth.

2 Draw in one large eye and a row of teeth.

you can do it!
Use crayons for texture and paint over it with watercolor paint. Use a felt-tip marker for the lines.

3 Add little hands and feet.

Splat-a-fact
This monster can hover in the air.

4 Draw in the horns and antennae.

23

Gizzard

1 Start with a long, curvy body. Add three eyes.

2 Add the mouth, teeth, ears, and hair.

you can do it!
Use colored pencils. Try putting textured surfaces under your paper to create interesting effects.

Splat-a-fact
This monster has seven legs and three eyes!

3 Draw in seven legs with circles for feet.

4 Add stripes, and draw in spikes and a heart-shaped tail.

Oddlin

1 Cut out this shape from colored tissue paper, and glue down.

Splat-a-fact
This monster likes to chase smaller monsters.

MAKE SURE YOU GET AN ADULT TO HELP YOU WHEN USING SCISSORS!

you can do it!
Cut the shapes from colored tissue paper, and glue in place. Use a felt-tip marker for the lines.

2 Draw in one eye, a mouth, and teeth.

3 Cut out the shapes for two large feet, and glue down.

4 Draw in two arms. Tear out pieces of tissue paper to decorate the body. Glue down.

Fijjit

1 Start with this shape and add two eyes.

2 Add details to the eyes and a line of sharp teeth.

3 Draw in the horns and finish off the mouth.

Splat-a-fact
Monsters can run super fast.

4 Add the arms and claws.

you can do it!
Use crayons for texture, and paint over it with watercolor paint. Use a felt-tip marker for the lines.

5 Draw the legs and feet.

Krungo

1 Start with a spiky body.

2 Add two dots for nostrils, a mouth, and teeth.

you can do it!
Use a felt-tip marker for the lines. Add color with oil pastels, and blend the colors with your fingers.

Splat-a-fact
This monster is great at climbing trees.

3 Add a striped horn, two eyes, and feet.

4 Add the arms and claws.

splazz

1 Start with this shape. Add a mouth.

2 Add three eyes.

you can do it!
Use a graphite pencil for the lines, and add color using watercolor paints.

splat-a-fact
Some monsters live underwater.

4 Add two arms.

3 Add jagged teeth, scales, a tail, and fins.

Prootle

1 Start with the head shape. Add a mouth and teeth.

2 Draw in three eyes, two horns, and two ears.

Splat-a-fact
Monsters can sleep with their eyes open.

you can do it!
Use a felt-tip marker for the lines, then use soft pastels for the colors and blend with your finger.

3 Draw in the body, and add lots of spots.

4 Draw in the arms and legs.

Bat

1 Start with the head shape.

2 Add angry eyes and a mouth with fangs.

3 Draw in two pointed ears.

4 Add two wings.

splat-a-fact
Bats are the only mammals that can really fly.

you can do it!
Use a felt-tip marker for the lines and then add color with watercolor paints. Dab on more color with a sponge to add texture.

5 Draw in two legs and feet.

Witch

1 Start with this shape for the head and hat.

2 Draw in the peak of the witch's hat. Add the warty nose, mouth, teeth, and angry eyes.

3 Add hair.

you can do it! Use crayons to create swirly textures and paint over it with watercolor paint.

4 Draw in the body and the feet.

5 Add the arms, hands, and a potion bottle.

38

Dragon

1 Start with a circle for the body.

2 Draw in this head shape.

3 Add angry eyes, ears, nostrils, and sharp teeth.

splat-a-fact
Dragons scare off evil spirits.

4 Draw in two front legs. and one back leg.

You can do it!
Use colored pencils. Put textured surfaces under your paper to create interesting effects.

5 Add a wing and a pointed tail.

40

Monster

1 Start with a box-shaped head.

2 Draw in the eyes, nose, and mouth.

3 Add ears, hair, stitches, and bolts on the neck.

4 Add the body. Draw a curved line and button for his jacket.

5 Draw in the arms with a circle for each hand.

you can do it!

Use oil pastels, and smudge them with your finger. Use a felt-tip marker for the lines.

6 Add legs, feet, and ragged trousers.

42

Ghost

1 Cut out a wavy shape for the body. Glue down.

2 Draw in a mouth, and add two dots for the eyes.

splat-a-fact
Ghosts haunt old, spooky houses and come out at night.

3 Cut out two waving arms. Glue down.

Igor

2 Add two dots for the eyes. Draw in a bandage, a nose, ears, a mouth, and teeth.

1 Start with an oval shape for the head. Add tufts of hair.

3 Draw a circle for the body, and add a belt

4 Add the arms with ragged sleeves.

you can do it!
Use a brown felt-tip marker for the lines and colored felt-tip markers to color in.

5 Draw in the legs and feet. Add trousers with ragged edges and a hole in them.

46

Mummy

1. Start with an oval for the head and dots for eyes.

2. Add bandages and a dot for the mouth.

3. Draw an oval for the body.

4. Add the arms.

5. Draw in two legs.

6. Draw in the mummy's bandages.

splat-a-fact
Mummies are wrapped in bandages and live in tombs.

you can do it!
Use crayons to create textures and paint over it with watercolor paint. Use a felt-tip marker for the lines.

Scarecrow

you can do it!
Use a felt-tip marker for the lines and watercolor paints for color. Add ink to the paint while it is still wet for added interest.

1 Start with an oval for the head. Draw a line through the middle.

2 Add eyes, a nose, a jagged mouth, and a stalk.

3 Draw in curved lines.

4 Draw in a jacket, belt, and frayed trousers. Add spiky straw feet.

5 Add two arms and straw hands.

Splat-a-fact
Scary faces are carved into pumpkins on Halloween.

50

Vampire

1 Start with a circle for the head, and add two ears.

2 Draw in a nose, a mouth, fangs, and dots for the eyes. Add eyebrows and hair.

3 Draw in the body and arms. Add collar and necklace detail.

4 Draw in the jacket, and add a cape.

5 Add legs and feet.

you can do it!
Use a felt-tip marker for the lines and colored pencil to color in using scribbly marks.

52

53

Werewolf

1 Start with this head shape.

2 Draw two angry eyes and nostrils. Add sharp teeth.

3 Add two front legs with furry paws.

4 Draw the back legs and bushy tail. Add a belt.

Splat-a-fact
Werewolves howl at the full moon.

54

Witch on broomstick

1 Start with the witch's face. Draw a line for the hat.

2 Add the pointed hat.

3 Draw in angry eyes, a mouth, and teeth. Add warts and hair.

4 Draw in the witch's tunic. Add arms and feet.

5 Add a broomstick.

You can do it!
Draw the outlines in a black felt-tip marker. Color in with colored pencils.

Witch's cat

3 Add a pointy hat and whiskers.

you can do it!
Add color with watercolor paint.

1 Start with an oval for the head. Add the chin.

2 Draw in the eyes, nose, and mouth.

splat-a-fact
Witches have cats to help them make their potions.

4 Draw in two overlapping ovals for the cat's body.

5 Add back and front legs and a curved tail.

59

Wizard

1 Cut shapes for the head and hat. Glue down.

2 Cut a shape for the face, and glue down. Add eyes and a mouth with a felt-tip marker.

Splat-a-fact

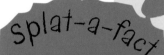

Wizards can turn people into frogs with magic spells.

3 Cut out a tunic shape and triangles for feet. Glue down.

you can do it!

As you cut out the shapes, glue them down onto colored paper. Cut out simple shapes to make a bat and a frog.

4 Cut out the sleeves, hands, a wand, and a staff. Glue down.

skeleton

1 Start with a skull shape.

2 Add eyes, a nose, and lines for the mouth.

3 Draw two ovals for the body. Add lines to one and two big dots to the other.

4 Add bone shapes for the arms and hands.

you can do it!
Color in with watercolor paint. Use a felt-tip marker for the lines.

splat-a-fact
The smallest bone of the human body is found in the ear.

5 Draw in bone shapes for the legs.

Index